The Chicago Defender and the Great Migration

by Kathleen Cox

Editorial Offices: Glenview, Illinois • Parsippany, New Jersey • New York, New York
Sales Offices: Needham, Massachusetts • Duluth, Georgia • Glenview, Illinois
Coppell, Texas • Ontario, California • Mesa, Arizona

CONTENTS

Slavery ended with the addition of the 13th amendment to the U.S. Constitution. As of December 18, 1865, every man and woman in the United States was free; the country had shaken off the shackles of slavery forever. The system that allowed one person to own another person was dead.

During the next five years, Congress passed two more constitutional amendments to shore up the liberties of African Americans. The 14th amendment granted them equal citizenship. The 15th amendment granted African American men the right to vote, a right they now shared with all other American men.

For the first time in their lives, African American men had the right to vote for leaders to represent them in government. For the first time in their lives, all African Americans had the right to earn money and the right to own land. The future of African Americans in the South seemed bright with promise.

A small portrait of Lincoln is included with this picture of a happy family celebrating the Emancipation Proclamation. Around it are scenes depicting slavery.

Before the Civil War it was illegal in some states to teach African Americans to read. Many learned this skill in schools for freed slaves following the Civil War.

Chapter 1 A Bright Hope Cut Short

African Americans were eager to take advantage of their new freedoms. Most of them did not want to be a **burden** on anyone. They hoped to get plots of land and become independent farmers. Some dreamed of starting businesses.

As former slaves began to take their first steps up the economic and social ladders, many white Southerners resented their progress. States in the South began to pass laws that robbed emancipated slaves of their new rights.

Slavery gave way to segregation—a new injustice. Segregation forced African Americans into a separate and unequal place in American society. White and black children attended separate schools. White and black people used separate entrances at public restaurants, theaters, and even circuses. Black people were expected to keep out of the way of white people.

The Ku Klux Klan struck terror in the hearts of African Americans, while segregation made them separate and unequal.

African Americans also suffered at the hands of the Ku Klux Klan (KKK). Southern white men created this organization to stop African American men from exercising their right to vote.

The Ku Klux Klan was a violent group. Members hid their identities under white masks and white sheets. Bands of these frightening men would ride on horseback and attack African Americans late at night. They set African Americans' homes on fire or broke into them and terrified their occupants. These white men did more than rob blacks of their constitutional rights. They fanned a flame of a hatred that spread across **rural** and **urban** areas.

Slavery had been a nightmare; but segregation was little better. The laws in Southern states were stacked against African Americans, and many lived in fear. They longed for a better life where they had a chance to fulfill their dreams. Many African Americans began to believe that this better life was beyond their reach in the South.

African American sharecroppers often found themselves in lifelong debt to those who owned the land they worked.

African Americans started emigrating from the South as soon as they won their freedom. Some headed to cities in the North; some headed to the wide-open spaces of the West. Leaving the South wasn't easy, however. It was expensive, and it was risky.

Many African Americans were sharecroppers—tenants who paid landowners a big share of their crops for the right to farm small plots of land. The white landowners often overcharged the tenants for seeds, supplies, and equipment. Often, sharecroppers had to borrow from landowners to pay these expenses.

Sharecroppers rarely made enough money to pay off these debts. Some tried to flee, but they were often caught and returned. Many paid with their lives.

Just before the turn of the twentieth century, the Supreme Court dealt another blow to African Americans. A majority of Supreme Court justices decided that the creation of separate facilities for blacks and whites did not violate the Constitution as long as the separate facilities were equal.

Chapter 2
One Man's Dream

African Americans knew that the phrase "separate but equal" was a lie. The places set aside for them were equal in name and nothing else.

Robert S. Abbott

Now, with the Supreme Court's ruling, segregated facilities in the South were given official approval. Separate and inferior schools would continue to exist. So would separate and inferior entrances, seating areas, drinking fountains, and everything else designed to keep African Americans separate from and unequal to white people.

In 1905, a well-educated African American in Chicago saw what was happening around him and formed his own special dream. He was determined to make it come true. Robert S. Abbott's parents had been born into slavery. Abbott, however, was a frustrated young lawyer. Because of the color of his skin, he was barred from practicing law in Indiana, Kansas, and Illinois.

At the age of 37, Abbott changed professions. He would not fight racism in the courtrooms, he decided. He would fight racism with paper and ink. He decided to become a newspaper publisher. He would show the world the power of the press.

Abbott realized his dream with an investment of 25 cents. He had no employees. He performed all the newspaper jobs himself. He became a reporter and set out to gather important local news and information that would interest his targeted audience—the African American community.

On May 5, 1905, he had enough material to put together the first issue of his new weekly newspaper. He was both the editor and the artist who designed each page. He sat at the kitchen table in his landlord's apartment and created *The Chicago Defender*. The newspaper was four pages long. Each page had six columns of articles.

Abbott became a publisher. He persuaded a printer to make 300 copies of his newspaper on credit. Then he became the entire sales force and the delivery man. He took the first edition of *The Chicago Defender* into Chicago neighborhoods and hawked them for two cents a copy. He also delivered copies to people who had promised to read his newspaper.

Abbott created a new American weekly that was unlike other African American newspapers. The former lawyer gave his people more than the news. It was Abbott's mission to help African Americans improve the quality of their lives. He also planned to reach an audience that lived far away from Chicago.

A newsboy selling *The Chicago Defender*, a leading African American newspaper during World War II

African American porters smuggled copies
of *The Chicago Defender* into the South.

Chapter 3 Spreading the Word

The Chicago Defender was an instant hit with its
readers. It became the first paper for African Americans
to sell more than 100,000 copies each week. It even
reached readers far beyond Chicago.

Getting the newspaper into different parts of the
country, especially the South, was not easy, however.
Many white Southerners thought an African American
newspaper from a Northern city spelled nothing but
trouble. Often distributors refused to sell *The Chicago
Defender* in the South. Ku Klux Klan members destroyed
all the copies they found.

Abbott turned to other African Americans for help.
At that time, railroads often employed African Americans
as porters. As many trains left Chicago, Illinois, for
southern states, black porters carried with them hidden
copies of *The Chicago Defender*. African American
entertainers who traveled between the North and the
South also carried copies with them.

African Americans eagerly read and discussed the news in *The Chicago Defender*.

Chapter 4
Reading *The Chicago Defender*

The number of readers of *The Chicago Defender* was much greater than the number of sales. In southern towns, African Americans shared single copies of the newspaper. They circulated it around their "Coloreds Only" barber shops and passed it around their churches. They often spent their **leisure** time reading it aloud to one another, discussing the articles and studying the pictures.

Each precious copy spoke directly to its target audience. Articles described violent attacks against African Americans. Editorials spoke out against racial injustice. A health column offered valuable advice. *The Chicago Defender* even had its own page of comics that appealed to African Americans.

The Chicago Defender also wisely **conformed** to the popular journalism of its time. It carried sensational headlines that made people eager to read all the gory details. It published vivid pictures.

The boll weevil destroyed cotton fields in the early 1900s, bringing more hardships to sharecroppers.

Chapter 5 Weather, Crops, and War

In the early 1900s, a series of events hit southern farmers hard. A terrible pest, the boll weevil, invaded the South. The fast-eating beetle wiped out entire cotton fields. Since cotton was one of the most important crops in the South, the boll weevil infestation affected both white and black farmers.

Meanwhile, the nation was dealing with another problem. In 1914, World War I broke out in Europe. In 1917, the U.S. government declared war on Germany. The United States was at war.

The war drew many men to Europe to fight, leaving positions open in many Northern factories.

The war halted the steady stream of workers who had been emigrating to the United States from Europe. At the same time, many American men quit their jobs in the cities of the North to answer the call of the military. They enlisted, put on a uniform, and went off to fight the war.

This left industries in the North with too many jobs and too few workers. Northern industries, including many companies in Chicago, had many jobs. Thousands of these positions were low-paying. They didn't demand high skills or even an education. All the same, they paid enough to cover the **maintenance** of a typical family.

Finally, the weather in the South also turned against farmers. A huge flood in 1927 destroyed many of the remaining crops that had continued to provide income to suffering farmers.

Many farmers, especially sharecroppers, lost everything they owned. To make things worse, whites who were ruined by these disasters took out their anger and frustration on black people. The Ku Klux Klan grew more powerful. Racial attacks increased. More and more African Americans wanted to leave the South.

Abbott realized that this economic picture offered the perfect opportunity for his people in the South. They could finally escape the hopeless trap of poverty and despair that came from a lifetime of racial injustice.

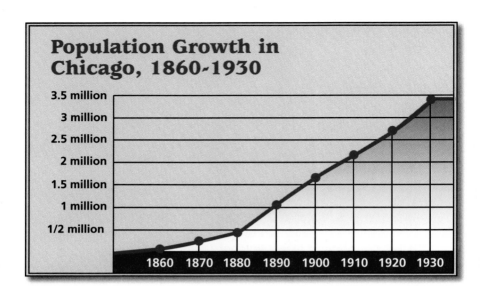

Population Growth in Chicago, 1860-1930

Chapter 6 The Great Migration

The newspaper publisher helped set in motion a movement known as the Great Migration. It took place between 1915 and 1930. Abbott also showed the white media the power of the black press.

Article after article in *The Chicago Defender* encouraged African Americans to migrate to Chicago. Stories compared the pleasures of urban life in the North with the despair of life in the South. The contrast was vivid.

For example, Abbott ran comparison photos of a school in Chicago next to a ramshackle school in the South. Any student or parent could see which school offered the better education.

In addition, *The Chicago Defender* ran interviews with African Americans who had recently made the move to Chicago. These migrants spoke highly about their new lives. They could move freely along Northern streets without getting insulted or threatened. In the North, Abbott implied, African Americans could throw back their shoulders and stand tall. They were free.

Many popular musicians became new members of Chicago's African American community. They, too, had responded to the call to migrate north that was repeated in issue after issue of *The Chicago Defender*. Jazz greats, such as piano player Jelly Roll Morton and cornet player Freddie "King" Keppard, boarded trains in New Orleans. First, they headed west, to Los Angeles. Eventually, they took seats in cars reserved for blacks only and looked forward to better days ahead in the urban North.

Once they reached their destination, they began to blend the Southern sound of New Orleans with a Northern sound created in Chicago.

The Chicago Defender boasted of the good times in the city. They told their readers about the jazz night clubs presenting talented African Americans. These musicians made them proud. They were the best! Even white people came to see them perform.

Jazz pioneer Jelly Roll Morton

All the migrants who were interviewed in *The Chicago Defender* spoke with enthusiasm about their new jobs. Yes, they told the paper, the cost of living was higher in the North, but they found good work there. Some worked in the railroad yards. Others worked in the steel mills and the stockyards. Many factories and industries were eager to hire new employees.

Many of them earned more than $2.50 a day. They made **sufficient** money to pay their bills. Even black servants working for white Chicago families made twice the amount of money they had made working for white families back in the South.

African Americans found work in northern factories, such as this foundry.

African Americans migrating to Chicago from the South had to get used to city life.

Chapter 7 Different Lifestyles

Many African Americans in the South lacked the courage to move to the North. They worried that they would have trouble adapting to a lifestyle so different from the one they had known all their lives. In the South, a slow pace governed the rhythm of the days. People might live in small, poor houses, but they had privacy.

They were accustomed to shopping in a few familiar stores where they knew the owners. There was only one local barber shop, one bank, and a single post office. Everyone went to the same church. African Americans in small towns usually knew everyone in their community.

In contrast, Chicago was a huge, crowded city of more than two million people! To get around, newly arrived migrants had to master a complicated transportation system of trolley cars. They had to adjust to apartment living. They had to accept less space and less privacy.

Children of migrants needed to get accustomed to city schools where they sat in rooms with many classmates. Teachers and most of the other pupils did not speak in a southern accent. The sound of the English language was different. New southern pupils had to listen carefully.

Even Chicago's weather was radically different from the weather in the South. The city had long, cold winters. Blustery winds often rolled off Lake Michigan and rattled the windows in buildings. Cold winds sent a chill through the body. Sometimes blizzards dumped piles of snow onto the streets and sidewalks. The temperature often dropped below freezing.

Childen of migrants attend 6th and 7th grades in this schoolroom on Flint River Farms in 1939.

THE EXODUS

NORTHWARD BOUND
(Photo by Johnston, Savannah, Ga.)

Laborers waiting for the third section of the labor trains northward bound on the outskirts of Savannah, Ga. The exodus of labor from the South has caused much alarm among the Southern whites, who have failed to treat them decent. The men, tired of being kicked and cursed, are leaving by the thousands as the above picture shows.

Chapter 8
The Chicago Defender Lends a Hand

Abbott understood all these fears. He knew African Americans needed help to make such a radical move.

He addressed many of these problems in *The Chicago Defender*. Each issue included practical information. Abbott printed schedules of trains headed to Chicago from various southern cities. He published classified ads for jobs in Chicago. He printed the names of Chicago churches helping emigrants find housing and work.

Abbott also encouraged people to migrate in groups. He published articles about migration clubs, which were sprouting up throughout the South. Many were started by church women to bring together people wanting to move to the North. Members of each club met and traded news and information—often from the paper. The clubs organized each leg of the complicated journey. Members built up their courage by making important decisions together.

Migration clubs found power in numbers. They bargained with railroad companies for group discount tickets. They attracted agents from northern companies who visited and offered jobs to members. Many companies were so eager for workers that they offered to pay for train tickets and all other trip expenses.

Although life was difficult for most African Americans in the South, and mistrust—even hatred—swirled around them, many still found it hard to pull up their roots and leave. Their families had lived in the South for generations. The southern lifestyle flowed through their blood.

Abbott kept up his crusade, however, in *The Chicago Defender*. His editorials warned of the dangers that stalked African Americans in the South. Shocking pictures and headlines echoed his point. They called attention to awful acts of brutality that were committed against the black southern minority.

African American writers, including Langston Hughes, Richard Wright, and Gwendolyn Brooks, were all published regularly in *The Chicago Defender.*

Gwendolyn Brooks

More than 110,000 African Americans moved to Chicago from the South between 1916 and 1918. Over 1 million left the South for the North between World War I and the Great Depression of 1929. By 1929, *The Chicago Defender* sold 250,000 copies every week.

For years to come, this outspoken weekly newspaper reminded African Americans that they were worthy of equality. It introduced them to inspiring writers such as poets Langston Hughes and Gwendolyn Brooks, and novelist Richard Wright. These writers shared the experiences, worries, and concerns of *The Chicago Defender* readers.

Abbott never stopped fighting for the rights of his people. He wrote editorials calling for the integration of sports teams and for better treatment of African Americans in the military. He wrote about the unfair treatment of his race wherever he saw it in the United States.

The man who first assembled his newspaper on a kitchen table changed the lives of thousands of African Americans who longed for justice and a decent life. Through his newspaper, people far from Chicago heard—and answered—his call. The smart businessman, who became a millionaire, fulfilled his dream.

Langston Hughes

Richard Wright

Glossary

burden *n.* something that is difficult to carry that can often be a great sense of worry

conformed *v.* behaved or acted in a similar way

leisure *n.* free time for oneself

maintenance *n.* support, livelihood, or upkeep

rural *adj.* relating to the country, farming, or agriculture

sufficient *adj.* enough or adequate

urban *adj.* relating to the city or city life